A Gym Owner's Blueprint
for Making More Money

THE ULTIMATE GUIDE TO
$ALES
FOR YOUR
GYM

Vince Gabriele, MS
Foreword By The Legendary Thomas Plummer

THE ULTIMATE GUIDE TO SALES FOR YOUR GYM
by
VINCENT GABRIELE

For information write to:
63 INDUSTRIAL ROAD
BERKELEY HEIGHTS NEW JERSEY 07922
908-464-4441
WWW.GABRIELEFITNESS.COM

CONTENTS

Dedication

For my incredible wife, Vanessa.

FOREWORD

The mainstream fitness business is a dying industry and it has left us an ugly legacy.

The big box fitness centers started big back in the 1960s. The owners of these facilities created much of what passed for business practices in the entire fitness business for over five decades.

These dated, and often shady, owners used hardcore sales tactics that alienated the clients. They used deceptive marketing that eroded the trust in even fitness itself. They created businesses they hoped you would never visit once they got your money. They failed to evolve and are still attempting to sell a version of fitness that is neither good for the client nor good for anyone else in the industry.

But there is a new generation of gym owners who represent the best of what fitness can and should be... and no one represents this new generation better than Vince Gabriele.

The fitness business fragmented in the early 2000s. The mainstream industry took the road to the bottom, turning fitness into a commodity sold by the cheapest provider to an unaware buyer who expected, and deserved, more from those businesses.

The other segment, a new species that had never existed prior in the industry, bet their future on a client who wanted real help, valued real coaches and would pay for the best in fitness in a good gym.

The new gym owner is passionate, creative, caring and focuses on doing what is best for the client each and every day. He or she lives and dies by getting maximum results from the maximum number of clients they serve.

This new generation came with passion, but often without the leadership necessary to run a financially successful business on a day-to-day basis. We have a thousand new gyms opening every year around the country owned by people who want to do the right thing, but who have not yet found the skills and business leadership needed to live their dream.

Vince Gabriele is providing that leadership to this generation of gym owners. He successfully opened his first small gym, worked his ass off for several years developing his product and service, and then expanded again, and again, finally evolving into one of the most successful training businesses in the country. Vince not only lived the dream, he discovered how to make money out of doing what he loves every single day.

One of the hardest skills for this new generation of gym owners to grasp is sales. Even the word itself has an ugly connotation. When we think of sales in fitness, we again think of the old mainstream players selling across a desk in a stuffy office using the sales tactics that would make an old-school used cars salesman blush.

In Vince's new book, he redefines sales for a new generation of owner who still must grasp the basic nuisances of having an educated conversation with a client and then being able to ask that potential client to become part of the business. Sales to Vince isn't pressure or negativity; sales is the ability to help the client get what he came into the gym for both professionally and ethically.

You must learn to help people who need your guidance and support, but first you have to answer their questions, guide them toward the right membership, price the gym for the market you serve, and finally be able to look the client in the face and say, "Sir, let's get you signed up today."

This book is one of a series of all the basic business skills you have to learn to run a financially successful gym business. These books are written by a guy who has been there, did the job, created a business that makes money and then, and only then, chose to write and speak about it. There are a lot of new books about the gym business, most written by guys who read someone else's book and then rip off the theme without ever understanding what it really takes to make money in a real gym.

The gym business is a difficult one. From the outside, it looks like a dream job, but inside it is a very intensive customer service nightmare serving clients with money who demand nothing but the best from you every day you are in business and your doors are open.

It also takes a truly experienced owner and good businessman, such as Vince, to capture only the necessary thoughts to be successful over time. You can be lucky for a while, but to be good over time means you have learned the basics of business and there is no better place to start then with Vince.

My first time through the book I laughed to myself thinking, "How could he get so much good information in such a tightly written book?" I read it again and realized it was the perfect read for the new generation gym owner. Everything you need to know about sales, no wasted crap that makes you want to put the book down, and strong action steps where you can put the book down and start being more effective at helping those clients get what they truly want from you and your business.

There is a new generation of gym guru out there now; men and women who are rebuilding the fitness industry into something built upon pride, effectiveness, professionalism and ethics and I believe Vince represents the best in all of these things.

Hope you enjoy this book as much as I did. He has a lot to teach you here, but if you pay attention, your business will be the better for it starting the next day.

Yours in fitness,
Thomas Plummer
October, 2018

INTRODUCTION

There's a massive problem among many gym owners.

Many are tired, stressed and thinking to themselves "what the hell did I get myself into?"

They jumped into owning their gym with both feet, gave everything they had and now all that's left is this cash-eating monster that they cannot seem to get under control.

They're losing steam

Gym owner burnout is a colossal problem in our industry

You probably go to seminars or conferences and see guys that own gyms that look like they haven't slept in weeks. Many of them are completely out of shape and almost all of them are stressed out.

They are still running their gym, but they aren't enjoying it – not by any means.

They're going through the motions, just trying not to go out of business.

I also know you've probably seen other gym owners just throw in the towel and sell their gym for nothing, or even just walk away because they were just fried.

They left a potential career filled with transforming lives, money and freedom for a 60-minute commute, a desk, a 9 to 5 and a paycheck.

They gave up freedom for certainty.

They gave up because the career they once loved turned to hate; hate from stress, uncertainty, fear and dealing with all kinds of issues they just didn't want to deal with.

Some of this may sound familiar to you. I know it does to me.

You're banging 40+ sessions per week.

You're working split shifts where you get to the gym at 5 AM and leave at 9 PM.

You're trying to learn how create systems, market, sell, build a team and look at financials all on the fly.

You're dealing with trainers that don't show up, and when they do, they're late and cranky.

You have clients that drain your energy, but you can't fire them because you can't afford to lose them.

You have other clients that pay the least and complain the most.

You're starting to lose focus on your own health.

You wake up exhausted at 4:30 AM and rely on caffeine just to get through the day.

When you get home, there is nothing more to give.

Life is usually happening at the same time, too:

- You get engaged.
- Then married.
- You buy a home.
- You have a child, and then another.
- You have to think about life insurance, college tuition and saving for retirement.

I only know this so well because I've been here.

I've lived through ALL of this.

I was once a burnt-out gym owner that was close to throwing in the towel

I was so close I actually asked my dad how to go about starting to work with him in the finance industry.

But I found the way out, and many of my clients have, too.

Succeeding as a gym owner is NOT easy.

But when you breakthrough, it will bring a life of freedom, happiness and prosperity.

I want to introduce you to a concept that will protect you from being a burnt-out gym owner and be the source of your breakthrough.

This concept will not only protect you but gives you something truly special: freedom so you can enjoy your life.

It's called **SPF** and it's your golden ticket to a successful, long-term career in the fitness industry.

SPF stands for Simple, Profitable and Fun.

Imagine your life if you ran a business that was simpler and easier.

Picture in your mind how your life would be if your gym was more profitable and you were able to see more money in your bank account.

When things are complex and money is not flowing, it's pretty hard to have any fun.

The Ultimate Guide Book Series for gym owners was created by a formerly burnt-out gym owner that found his way out, built a business that is Simple, Profitable and Fun and now lives a life of freedom and prosperity.

Much talk is in the industry is about lead generation, and rightfully so. That is why my first book, the Ultimate Guide to Marketing Your Gym, was first.

But solely generating leads does not put money in the bank.

The sales process is what actually rings the register.

The pages that follow give you a blueprint for a sales process that is guaranteed to make your gym more money and be a key piece of the equation to develop a gym that's SPF.

So, sit up in your chair in a peak state and devour the pages that follow – they're sure to put a lot more money in your pocket!

CHAPTER 1:
THE SALES MINDSET: WHY YOU NEED TO BE GOOD AT SALES

Sales Mindset #1: Your Financial Security

"I'm not in it for the money, I just want to be able to pay the bills and do what I love."

This is a line I hear quite often from gym owners that are struggling to make the amount of money they want.

This is usually stated by gym owners that may live with their parents, are under 25, and do not have children, a mortgage or a spouse.

But let's ask the gym owner that's 35 years old, has 3 kids, a wife and a house about money, and I am 100% certain he'd say that it matters quite a bit.

If you're not already, you'll be that 35-year-old sooner than you think.

Even if you're still young, you want to make as much money as you can because the more you save now, the better you'll be later.

The average personal training gyms makes about $300,000 annually in gross revenue.

In many parts of the country, after you strip away expenses and taxes, that's not a lot of money to live off.

Over the course of this book, I'm going to take you down the sales highway and through the end game of being great at sales and making more money.

That's really what this book is about: making more money.

I talked about my dad in my last book.

He suffered a very bad stroke and has lost his ability to speak, understand and move.

My father needs 24-hour aid care, and if I shared the monthly cost with you it would make your stomach turn.

These were supposed to be the golden years for my parents. They're supposed to be enjoying this time traveling and playing with their grandchildren, not spending their life savings on aid care and speech therapy.

The reality is that we do not know what life has in store.

We may need to hire a private tutor or send our kid to private school because they have a learning disability.

We may need to replace the boiler on our home for $15,000.

We may run into a recession and lose 50% of our members.

One of our trainers could take half of our members and set up shop down the street.

A family member may come into hard times and ask us for money.

You just don't know.

When you shine the light on situations like this, I cannot imagine not being able to help the people in need, especially the ones closest to you.

So, the first part of having a sales mindset is that you must embrace being good at sales simply for your own security and the security of your family.

Money is freedom and a being good at sales is the most important part of making money.

Sales mindset #2: People Need You

The belief that the people in your community that are not members of your gym are NOT in a position to transform their lives.

What you do truly matters. You literally save lives.

The mindset that there are many people in your community that truly need your gym to save their lives puts sales in a different perspective.

If we are not good at sales, people will go down the street for a cheaper option and will probably get injured from bad personal training.

They may try it on their own and then stop after 3 months, or they just continue doing nothing.

None of these options put them in a position to change their lives.

The same people that said they are not about the money will probably say they are all about helping people.

Being good at sales is how we help.

We cannot help anyone if they don't buy.

People need what we do, and you must believe in your gym so much that you believe if they do anything else except train at your gym, they are not safe.

The way to envision this is to picture your gym in the middle of the ocean.
There is a series of buoys set up in a circle that signify it.

The people inside the circle are your members, and they are safe.

They all have life vests on.

The water inside the circle is calm and there are lifeguards all around.

There are nets blocking any sharks from coming inside the circle, too.

The people outside the circle do not have life vests on.

They do not have access to lifeguards, the water is rough and there are no nets.

These people need to be saved.

It's your duty to get as many people inside your circle as possible.

CHAPTER 2:
THE THINGS STANDING IN THE WAY OF A SALE

When I was in 4th grade, I was on the local pool tennis team. I was the worst on the team and was partnered with the other worst player – I'll call him John.

For some reason, I could not stand John. I was a pretty laid-back kid and did not have many enemies, but John just totally irritated me.

One very hot summer day we were playing a match and getting crushed. John was up to his normal antics: throwing his racquet and yelling at me and our opponents for making bad calls (there were no judges for second doubles).

I had enough.

It was my turn to serve and I threw the ball in the air and hit it as hard as I could...right into the middle of John's back.

He turned and looked at me like "what the hell, man?"

I was like, "sorry, dude."

Man, it felt good to smash him, so I did it again.

John knew this one was on purpose, and so did everyone else that was there.

He went crazy.

He charged after me with his racquet and the fight was ultimately broken up by one of the nearby tennis pros.

They made us sit out, basically a time-out, which, when I think about it now, is hilarious.

We got back to the match and it was my turn to serve again.

Yup, you guessed it.

Smack! Right in the back. John held back from chasing me but now he was on the defense.

Every time I served, he would quickly turn his head to make sure the ball would not hit him.

It was like clockwork.

Toss the ball up to serve, John turns his head.

Toss the ball up, John turns his head.

He had lost total trust in me and feared I was going hit him with the ball every time.

John was definitely a jerk, but I certainly was one too that day.

So, how does this apply to sales?

Fear is the #1 thing standing in the way of making a sale.

This is VERY important: people want to buy, but they are afraid to buy.

There are 3 possible things causing this fear:

1. Betrayal from previous experiences.
2. A lack of confidence in themselves.
3. They don't want to feel dumb.

Betrayal from Previous Experiences

People have been betrayed many times by people that have tried to help them get results.

They've tried Weight Watchers and failed.

They've gone to the local personal trainer and failed.

They've joined the big box gym and never went.

They bought home exercise equipment that promised to melt their fat away and never even took it out of the box.

People want to be helped, and they want to buy.

If they didn't want to buy, they would not have tried so many things in the past.

We simply underestimate the number of times people have been hit in the back with a tennis ball.

We underestimate the doubt that people have when they walk through our door.

A Lack of Confidence in Themselves

After owning a gym for 11 years, I have had very few people terminate their membership saying that our program does not work.

When we have surveyed why people are not happy with results, the answer is almost always their own lack of discipline to eat right and get to the gym more often.

We are in an interesting situation where the results we get with our clients is largely out of our hands.

We can have the best program in the world, but if they don't show up and don't eat well or get enough sleep they probably won't be happy with their results.

At the end of the day, people know they are the reason they have not succeeded, and that feeds their lack of confidence in themselves.

They Don't Want to Feel Dumb

I am not very handy. I feel bad for my wife sometimes and think she thinks to herself "I need to get a real man that can fix stuff around this house."

When our drain gets clogged, it takes me a long time to call the plumber.

I will deal with it much longer than I should to avoid the pain of the guy showing up, charging me 300 bucks, and telling me I just needed to put some Drano in there.

What seems so easy to him is like Greek to me and I feel dumb.

Using a cable machine in the gym for us is like nothing, but the non-gym guy thinks you need a certification from NASA to use it.

So, he just doesn't use it because he does not want to feel dumb.

We must know that people actually feel like this and that it causes fear.

Until we show we are different than all the rest, we are in the same category as everyone else.

The job of the sales process is to demonstrate how, this time, it's going to be different.

This time, they are not going be hit in the back with a tennis ball.

Know, Like and Trust

If you could sum up the thing that gets people to buy, it would be getting your potential members to know, like and trust you.

I know this is a book about sales, but this really starts with your marketing.

It's rare that a customer calls a personal training gym without knowing you at all.

Most of the time they are seeing things from you either on social media, email, an event or in the mail, usually multiple times, before they decide the start a relationship with you.

KNOW

The *know you* part is making sure you are being consistent with your marketing message.

If you use Facebook, posting once every other week probably won't help them get to know you quickly.

Consistence and speed are key elements to help people get to know you quicker. Too many people wait for everything to be perfect before they put it out there.

I will take speed over perfection any day of the week. I'm not saying you should put out garbage, not even close, but too many gym owners work too slow.

The only people that care about an occasional typo in my emails are my mother and sisters (sorry guys).

We do our best to catch everything but when we're pushing the envelope to get our community to KNOW us, there may be an occasional mistake.

Another way to get people to know you is to make sure you are incredible with follow-ups once they contact you. There will be a monster chapter in this book on lead conversion, and even sales guru Grant Cardone says that sales success is all in the follow-up.

LIKE

You cannot be boring and get many people to like you.

"Don't be boring," says legendary marketing expert Dan Kennedy.

Your business needs to have a personality. One of our

core values at GFP is to have fun. You'll see us posting videos of ourselves dancing in the gym, for example. We always dress up for Halloween and we are always putting stuff out there that makes people laugh.

The 3 key components of our content marketing strategy are to educate, inspire and entertain.

Some people like to be motivated, others value information that helps them and some people just want to be entertained.

Following these 3 principles is a way to get people to like you without even meeting them.

TRUST

The trust part happens most effectively when you meet people in person.

That being said, you can start earning trust by doing little things before they even meet you.

Using testimonials in your marketing is one way to start that trust process earlier.

People see someone that had the same problems they have and that your gym was the place the helped them.

The trust factor normally comes from the way you make people feel. When people feel genuinely cared for, trust will be built. The upcoming chapter will dive deep into this.

CHAPTER 3:
THE NEW ABCS OF SELLING

"The leads are weak? You're weak."

–Alec Baldwin, from Glengarry Glen Ross

If you're in sales you need to see the movie Glengarry Glen Ross, especially the famous scene where he literally annihilates a team of sales people for their poor performance.

In that scene, he talks about the ABCs of selling:

- **A**lways
- **B**e
- **C**losing

As great as the movie scene is, however, it's simply not ALL about the close anymore.

It's not that the close is not important – it is. It's just that if you do everything right beforehand, the close is not the most important aspect of sales.

Dan Pink introduced me to the new ABCs of selling in his great book To Sell is Human.

He talks about how there used to be an imbalance in information between the buyer and the seller. When you showed up to buy a car, the seller knew everything, and the buyer knew nothing.

Times have changed. We are in an information-rich world and there's as much information available to the buyer as the salesperson.

Think of it this way: you have knowledge about how to eat to get lean as well as the best exercises to burn fat.

As a trainer, you have that expertise.

But if one of our clients wanted to learn that as well, they are just a Google or YouTube search away.

The NEW ABCs of selling take this into consideration.

Here they are:

1. Attunement: the ability to see things through the eyes of the other person.
2. Buoyancy: the ability to stay afloat amongst an ocean of rejection.
3. Clarity: the ability to weed through all the information out there and show people what truly matters.

Attunement

As a young trainer, I often got frustrated with lazy moms. They would sit there and tell me how busy they were, yet they didn't have a job and only had to look after a few kids. It drove me crazy when they drank too much wine, ate chocolate after the kids went to bed and would go an entire day without eating, using only Starbucks to fuel their day.

My thoughts were "this lady is just plan lazy." Then I had had 3 children. I saw first-hand what my wife was dealing with and it wasn't easy. I know this because the few times my wife has been away, and I had all three kids for an extended time period, I was ready to drink, too.

Seeing this allowed me to have much more empathy for moms. It enabled me to see things through their eyes and not my own.

The Old Sales Proverb goes something like this:

If you can see John Smith through John Smith eyes, you can sell John Smith what John Smith buys.

Putting yourself in the shoes of the potential members that sit in your office will force you to ask more questions and be a much better listener.

Asking questions and listening gets you to the heart of the most important part of the sales process: people telling you want they want.

When I get on the phone to help a gym owner just starting out, I need to put myself in their shoes. It always helps me because while I have walked in their shoes, if I tried to help them with where I am today after an 11-year career as a gym owner, I would not be effective as a coach.

Two ears and one mouth

One of the most important parts of attunement is listening. If you've ever read the book *How to Win Friends and Influence People*, one of their main pillars for influencing people is being a great listener.

Great listeners are hard to come by these days.

Here are a few things that keep people from being good listeners.

1. Being in a hurry.

One of the biggest challenges for gym owners starting out is that they squeeze sitting down with potential new customers in between all the other stuff they have going on. They are showing up to sales meetings knowing they have exactly 30 minutes before their next class starts. Even worse, they squeeze in a workout before the meeting and show up out of breath and sweaty to a sales meeting. This is the process that makes the money and it's hard to do well if you're in a hurry. The people will feel it and it certainly won't put your best foot forward.

2. Inability to stay focused.

There is nothing more important than the person in front of you at that moment, aside from an extreme emergency. Using smart phones and always being tuned into technology has impaired our ability to have genuine conversations where we are engaged in truly listening to what people are saying.

3. Being a waiting to talker.

I must credit the great Steve Shenbaum for this. A "waiting to talker" is the person that makes it completely obvious that they are simply waiting for you to finish what you're saying and will only be whole when they get their words out. Steve has a very funny way of demonstrating this, but I can spot them a mile away.

Learning to be a great listener is a key skill to being great at sales. This is how you will be able to put yourself in the other person's shoes. If you don't listen enough to learn about what they want, it will be hard to get on their level.

Here are a few listening basics.

1. Eye Contact

I was at the gas station the other day and had a 10-minute conversation with the side of a man's face. He was a guy I had known years ago, and we were catching up while my tank was filling up. No exaggeration, he never looked at me. He stood facing toward the back of my truck and we had a normal conversation but the only thing I could notice was where he was looking and how awkward it was. It was almost like he was staring at the gas pump that was inserted in my truck and never wanted to stop looking at it. It was so weird. That's the only thing I remember, but I am also pretty sure anything I said to him during that time, he didn't hear. Making eye contact shows that you're genuinely interested in what people are saying.

2. Body Language

I once got interviewed by a guy that wanted me to talk about my experience running a gym.

He would ask me a question then would have this fidgety body language that communicated to me "ok, I'm ready for you to be done now." It was so distracting to me and it affected the quality of my answers.

66 % of communication is non-verbal and body language is a massive part of that. Having good posture and positive body language is a key ingredient to good listening.

3. Active Listening

It's always a little weird to talk and receive no response from the other side to confirm they are still alive. I was on a podcast once and told what I thought was a funny story, and the guy didn't say a word. Either I overestimated how funny the story was or he was asleep – or he just didn't practice good listening skills.

When someone is talking, confirming you are hearing what they're saying with phrases like "really? That's awesome! Wow. That's crazy! I'm so sorry. Oh man," and nodding your head are key.

This confirms you are engaged in the conversation and genuinely interested in what they're saying, which will bring you closer to building a rapport with them.

4. Write Notes

We are going to unpack the consultation process in a later chapter, but taking notes during a consultation type situation is a must and only confirms to the person that you are genuinely interested in what they're saying.

5. Know What You're Listening For

To achieve attunement and move the sales process forward, there are some key factors that you need to listen for to help get on their level.

1. What is keeping them up at night? Taking pain away is a massive advantage in sales.

2. What do they worry about most? Their worries are the most impactful motivators.

3. What is most important to them? This can be long term health, losing weight, getting out of pain, improving strength, relieving stress, etc.

These will be brought out by the line of questioning in a later chapter, but it's crucial to be aware when these important factors come up and to bring them up later in the sales process to connect them with your program.

Buoyancy: The ability to stay afloat amongst an ocean of rejection.

LLOYD
What are my chances, Mary?

MARY
Not good.

LLOYD
Like one out of 100?

Mary
More like one in a million.

Lloyd
{Long Pause}
So you're telling me there's a chance!
Yeahhh!!!!

This is from a scene from one of my favorite movies, *Dumb and Dumber.*

When I lived in San Diego, the first day on the job as an intern at Fitness Quest 10, they introduced me to one of their Pilates instructors.

She was the most beautiful girl I had ever seen. I had just started the internship with another guy and we both were like "dude, did you see that Pilates instructor? Damn!"

He pushed hard to try to go out with her many times. No

dice. He quit soon after.

I kindly asked her to go to dinner one night after work, but nothing doing.

I invited her to my house for a party, but she was busy.

One night I got really drunk with her and we kissed, but the next day she swore nothing happened.

After several more months of rejection, I asked her to go to a Tom Petty concert.

She said, "Who's that?"

But something in her went.

11 years later this beauty and I are happily married with 3 children.

Not everyone will sign up for your gym.

In fact, it's a great month when we close 6 out of 10 potential members to an annual membership.

If we were in school, that would be a D-.

If this was baseball, we'd have the highest batting average ever recorded by 200%!

Some people just don't have the money.

Others did not connect with you.

Many will just lack the motivation to take the next step.

The most successful sales people are the ones that learn

from the times they do not make a sale, not those that swim in a sea of sorrow.

Buoyancy is all about not being affected by the word "no."

It's a hard concept to grasp but being excited by failure is what really needs to be done.

No, you don't want to try to lose, but if you do your absolute best and still fail there are lots of lessons to be learned.

The way I have built this strategy into my life is by adopting something called a growth mindset.

I learned this from the great book, Mindset, by Carol Dweck.

It talks about two different ways to view things like failure, criticism and challenges.

With a fixed mindset you are defined by the result. So, when you fail, you view yourself as a failure.

With a growth mindset, you are focused on the process.

You are focused on the effort that was put in, and, if the result was not desirable, what information can be taken to grow and improve.

It's been life-changing to think this way, but it takes time. Some people are more wired than others toward a growth mindset, but everyone can learn to think this way.

All this being said, if you put yourself in front of the right people, sales can be so much easier and you will be more successful than you thought.

This is especially true for when you delegate the sales process (which, in my opinion, is one of the last things to give up).

You most likely will take personal trainers that are inexperienced sales people and expect them to know how to sell. They don't. But they can still do well if they are continually put in front of very warm prospects.

Think about the last time you sat down with a referral from one of your best members.

They came in knowing about you from their friend who has sung your praises and they are in the same social circle of your affluent client.

This person does not take a lot of sales skill to close and I have sold people like this a $6,000 membership after one meeting.

Getting in front of the right people really comes back to your marketing.

If you haven't already, download a FREE copy of my first book, The Ultimate Guide to Marketing Your Gym, at www.ultimategymguide.com.

Clarity:

I picked up an issue of *Men's Health* magazine the other day and something on the cover really caught my eye.

It read "792 cool new health, fitness, sex and style tips."

792? Are we supposed to implement these all in the same week?

People do not lack information.

People lack two things:

1. A clear plan for success – a strategy.
2. Finding the right problem to solve.

Helping people develop a strategy is one way you can differentiate yourself.

You will win when you simply make things easier for people in a world where everyone is making things more complicated

"Complexity is the enemy of execution." – Tony Robbins

If you try to compete as the most technical trainer out there, you will struggle. You probably know enough exercises right now to last you a lifetime. I have been to countless seminars where I used .01 percent of what I learned, if that much.

People lack the knowledge about what they need to do next.

I will be introducing our health road map that we use with every member at GFP in a later chapter.

The roadmap is basically everything someone needs to do to get healthy on one page. It's a very powerful tool that brings clarity to people's lives.

Finding the Right Problem to Solve

The classic example of "this is what we know about the human body." Usually, if someone comes to you with a bad lower lack, if you have any real knowledge, you will just strengthen the area.

You probably know to look at their hips or their thoracic spine as the causes of the pain.

You probably will look at lifestyle habits. Are they under a ton of stress, are they sitting for 8 hours a day, etc.

The pain is in the back, but that is not the cause.

Many people need someone to help them find the real thing that will help them.

For instance, I had a guy come into my office recently who was really stressed out. After one look at his breathing pattern, I knew the way he was breathing was a major issue, but it was something he didn't even consider.

People need someone to help them find the right problem to solve.

When your sales process consists of things like this, you'll be on the winning team.

CHAPTER 4:
BOOK MORE CONSULTS AND MAKE MORE MONEY

I recently inquired about getting hyperbaric treatments for my dad, who suffered a pretty bad stroke about a year ago.

It's been a crazy time in my life, but I managed to get some free time and researched people in the area that provided this service.

I would do anything and spend any amount of money to get my dad talking again.

I have heard that hyperbaric chambers have produced some great results in stroke patients, but there are also many other options for secondary treatment.

I called the hyperbaric chamber place and the person I needed to speak with was not there, so I left a message.

They called back.... once.

In this crazy whirlwind, there have been so many people saying I need to try this and that to help my dad. It's been somewhat overwhelming and hard to keep track of it all.

I've looked at stem cells, peptides, acupuncture, special supplement protocols, vegan diets, Xi Gong, neurofeedback, etc.

I was ready to give the hyperbaric a chamber a chance.

But they never followed up with me again.

If they did, I would have taken him.

I just moved on to other things, not because I didn't think it would work and not because I didn't want to try it, but because it just fell off my radar.

When people pick up the phone and call you, they are the most likely to schedule an initial appointment in that moment.

If they had answered the phone and put me on with the right person, I would have booked an appointment that day, no doubt in my mind.

But now we are nowhere.

They don't have a client.

I don't have a solution for my dad.

These days of instant gratification, people want an immediate solution. If you do not respond either immediately or follow-up persistently in the first 4 days of the contact, they will most likely just let it fall off their radar, just like I did.

This is a massive problem with gym owners, and, quite frankly, most businesses in general.

This chapter is the solution to this issue.

Here are a few stats to whet your appetite:

- 78% of leads that convert will do so with the first company that calls them back.

- 33% of all leads get an email but no phone call.

- 80% of all leads received too few calls.

- 35% are contacted on the first call, 72% on the second call – but 48% never get a second call.

Statistic taken from research done by a company called speak to leads. I have used this service before and to be honest, for us, it was NOT successful for several reasons. This being said, the use of presenting these findings are to drive home the point that lead follow-up is a very important system and not many are doing it well.

What is considered a lead?

A lead is a person that raises their hand and says they're interested in something you have to offer.

It could be someone that calls you, emails you, private messages you, opts in for a lead magnet, walks in... you get the point.

That's what a lead is, and the sales process starts as soon as that contact is made.

This is where massive mistakes are made.

The mistake is looking at this exchange as a checklist item for an admin person.

You hired that admin, stuck them with one of the most

important jobs in your business, gave them no training, scripts or strategies to be successful, and wonder why things seem a little off.

Define the Desired Outcome

The number one thing you need to do is define what you want the end result to be from any lead that contacts you.

For example, our number one thing is to book a consultation – that's it. It's not to tell them everything about our business and it's not to try to sell them a membership. The only result I want from that first contact is to book a consultation.

Now, that's my personal goal and you may desire a different result, but ask yourself this: what is the desired outcome for that first contact? Oftentimes, the answer to that question will solve a lot of problems.

Script this Out

When gym owners hear the word script, they often think of a robotic telemarketer reading from a large binder. A well-executed script should feel just like a good conversation.

The reason why scripts are important in the sales process is because you are trying to create predictable, reliable results.

If you do not follow a version of a script, you leave one of the most important components of your entire business up to chance and you have no clue how to make it better.

So it's up to you to build something that is successful... then delegate it to an admin.

Once that admin is using your strategy, you can see how they are executing the plan YOU put in place.

There are so many different situations and each of them have their own variation, so I will just use the phone call as my example here.

The first part of the script is how you answer your phone.

It pains me when I call a gym and the tone of the person that answers is "why are you bothering me?"

They say the name of the gym really fast, in a less than friendly tone, and wonder why they cannot pay their rent.

You have 7 seconds to make a great first impression and how you answer the phone must be scripted, practiced and monitored.

Fun Fact: smiling when you talk changes the shape of your vocal chords and makes you sound happier. My team hates it when I call them out on this, but it definitely makes you sound more welcoming. Give it a shot!

Some business go as far as saying something like "it's a wonderful day at ABC company, how can I help you?"

While this is great, and I know some very successful businesses that do it, we have not taken this approach.

We simply say the name of our gym and then say who we are.

It sounds like this: "Gabriele Fitness, this is Vince."

Either way, you need to have a consistent way to answer the phone and be SURE that the tone of the person answering is friendly, warm and welcoming, no matter who your target market is.

No one is impressed by a lack of friendliness and common courtesy, and as stated above, no one wants to feel stupid.

I once called a fitness equipment company very early in my career before I started using Perform Better for everything I put in my gym.

I was asking about a very expensive piece of equipment that was a huge investment for me. I remember how stupid the guy made me feel when I was asking questions about it.

That's the ONLY thing I remember about that company, and I have never used them again and never will.

Too bad one phone call lost them an 11-year client.

The second part of the script is building rapport.

We always ask people how they heard about us.

This starts a conversation that takes them away from any fear they may have.

For example, if they mention that one of their friends who is a member of ours told them about us, that's a great opportunity to simply start a nice conversation about a person we have in common. It lets their guard down and makes it a conversation instead of a transaction.

This is why, in addition to a script, you need a nice, friendly person answering your phone.

Once a rapport is built, the second part needs to ask the about what they are looking to accomplish.

Too many people make the mistake of explaining what they do at this point.

People don't care about what you do, they care about what they want.

If you go into your pitch about you programming for small group training, you'll lose them.

So far, the script is:

1. Answer the phone nicely.

2. Ask them how they heard about you.

3. As them what they are looking to accomplish.

It's not a long drawn out script, it's simply asking some great questions.

The key is to get them talking about what they want.

Most businesses do not do this because they don't understand that it's not about them, it's about what the potential clients wants.

This puts you at a huge advantage right off the bat.

Here is our response after they spend time talking about what they want:

Please note: this is the exact process we use at GFP and the process we teach to our mastermind members. Your response here will vary on several decisions you make, but you may consider using some that work pretty damn well. ☺

"Awesome! Thanks so much for sharing all that. We would love to be the people to help you accomplish your goal.

Step 1 is coming in to meet with one of our coaches for our road map session.

They'll ask you a few more questions about your goals and your nutrition, watch you move around a little bit and will even help you create a roadmap so you can achieve exactly what you're looking for.

At that point, if we feel it's a fit to work with each other, the way to get started is with our 30-Day Jumpstart. We will go over all the details when you come in. The investment for the trial is $299, is that within your budget?

I have an available time from 10 AM-11 AM this Wednesday with Matt, does that work for you?

Awesome! I will be sending you an email confirming this session after we get off the phone. It will tell you everything you need to know.

Notice there is not a ton of info given about the program. We want the majority of the conversation to be spent by them answering questions and we don't want, nor do they want, to be on the phone for an hour. The goal here is to book the appointment. That's it.

If They Ask About Price Over the Phone

When someone asks about the price after the trial over the phone, many people just start reading off every price they have.

The problem here is that you have not built the value of any of those prices. They have not met your team, seen your gym, learned about your program or gotten the feeling that your place is different.

It's possible to do some of this in your marketing, but in my experience most gym owners don't have that kind of skill in that area.

Since you have not had the opportunity to effectively build the value of what do you and connect it with their needs and wants, it's just left to how the potential customer feels about the various amounts of money you give them.

With that being said, my advice is to use the following answer:

"We have several different price points ranging from x to Y. The best way to see which of our programs is the right fit for you is to come in for a consultation."

If your lowest price point is too expensive for them, you just prequalified them and they most likely were just shopping price.

For most personal training gyms, price shoppers are not the type of members that usually fit our model so this answer will save you some time.

Getting Rid of Tire Kickers Faster

Here is a strategy to get rid of tire kickers a little faster. We have a lead criteria sheet we use with our mastermind members that is beyond the scope of this book, but I will talk about one brief aspect. We use a color scheme to judge how qualified a lead actually is.

When we get a red lead (the lowest qualified people), there are usually a few qualities that put them in the red category:

1. They are from a town that is outside of the typical drive time (30 min+).
2. The area they live is in a low demographic area that is outside of your targeting radius.
3. They ask about price immediately.
4. They have no connection at all to any of your members.

In this case, we will sometimes just quote them a very high investment over the phone and not even offer the trial.

Some may view this as harsh, but I view it is being focused on the market you decided to serve. Every moment you spend with the wrong customers is time away from helping the right ones.

Normally if we do not close a lead, they are put into a follow up system. The red leads are not put into that system.

If you're doing a good job marketing these are rare, but they do occasionally occur.

Prequalification

The price of your trial membership also serves as a prequalification tool. For example, the current trial membership price for 30 days with us is $299.

When someone is willing to invest $299 for 30 days of training they are prequalifying themselves to be able to afford what you do.

There is no science behind the price of the trial. We have used $99, $149, $299 and $499. All have worked, some better than others, but it will be different for you.

My advice: test. Try several different price points and see what works best. If you can hit your lead and trial goal with a higher trial price point, you will actually make money on the front end, which is nice. That being said, if the price point of the trial is a deterrent then you may need to adjust.

What Happens After You Book the Consultation

What happens after you book a consultation is a massively important step that almost no one does well.

You always need to refer back to chapter 2.

People are fearful.

Booking a consultation does not mean they are going to show up!

The first thing you are doing is building trust.

When you book the consult, you should tell them you will be sending them an email that will explain everything they need to know about their consultation.

Simply saying you are going to send them that email and then following through is building trust.

The Confirmation Email

A few years ago, someone told me about flotation therapy. It is where you lie in a large tank filled with Epson salt and you float.

It is supposed to help with many things, including improved brain function, something I am always looking for.

When I looked online, I saw that it was basically a large coffin. I am somewhat claustrophobic and lying in a pool of salt water with the top closed was very scary.

I had a ton of thoughts running through my mind:

- Did I go in naked?
- How do they clean that thing?
- Do I HAVE to close the top or can I leave it open?
- What if the salt gets in my eyes?
- Is there anyone else in the tank or is just me?

After I booked my appointment, they sent me an email that answered every one of my questions.

I had this sigh of relief when I read the email and although I was still a little nervous, I went the appointment and loved it. I still float a few times a quarter today.

Once people book a consultation with you to come to your gym, they have these same thoughts running through their mind:

- Are they going to pinch my fat?
- Do I have to get on the scale?
- Are they going to crush me on the first day?
- What should I wear?
- Is everyone else going be in great shape?

Failure to ease people's minds from the booking to the time they show up is a massive mistake.

Do NOT assume that just because they book a consultation that they will actually attend the consultation.

THE MAGIC IS IN THE FOLLOW-UP!

People scheduling a consultation and not attending is a major problem that I spend a lot of time working on with my mastermind members.

Your confirmation email should explain exactly what is going to happen.

If you want to take it a step further like we have, send a video from the person that will be holding the consultation so they know who they will be meeting with and what will happen.

Finally, if you want to improve the rate of people that actually attend your consultation, tell them what to do if they need to reschedule or cancel.

It's very frustrating when you book and pay a trainer to run a consultation and they don't show up.

People don't look at it this way. They look at it like the consult was free and I just got busy or too scared to attend.

They do not think that there is another human being, a real person, that blocked an hour of their life and was expecting them

But they need to. They need to know.
Here's what to say. You can say this when you book the consult over the phone and in your email or video confirmation.

Lastly, as we have booked this on Matt's schedule from 10-11 AM this Tuesday, if for some reason you need to reschedule this appointment, please give is a call so we can give this appointment to another person.

It's also a very effective strategy to send a text message/ email or phone call reminder the day before the appointment.

Want access to the exact script we use?
Visit www.ultimategymguide.com/salesbook

What if they don't show up?

Even after you pull off every magic trick in the book, there will be a small percentage of people that either no-show or cancel a free consultation. I view these as two very different categories.

The person that calls to reschedule is the easiest. They give you ample time to give that hour to another person, which means they respect your time. They also show their continued interest because they went forward and rescheduled the appointment. This is the best-case scenario.

Then there are the people that simply don't show up. I have little patience for these kinds of people and they only get one mulligan with us. If they no-show to the appointment, we call them immediately (it must be right away).

The tone of our email is not one of frustration, but one of concern. We show genuine concern that something could be wrong that caused them to no-show/no-call to an appointment that was booked, confirmed and reconfirmed.

Best case here is they are either bad with time and forgot, which does happen, or they actually had an emergency.

When they do not get back to us, we put them on a lead follow-up list where we have a built-in system for how and when we will follow-up with them. We will book them another consultation but if they no show again, they are blacklisted.

The Forced Show Up

Karen Nitti, who is our director of operations and person behind the success of booking consultations, did something amazing just the other day.

There was a girl that had a consultation that called, literally 10 minutes before, to move her time. She re-booked for the next day and tried to do the exact same thing.

Karen basically told her she has to come as we have reserved a coach for her two times in the last two days. The girl paused, said "ok I will move something around and I'll be there."

She showed up and signed up, hence the forced show up and close. ☺

One key point here. This person happened to be a recent

college grad that had trained with us in the past, so there was a relationship in place.

This is not a structured system we use, but the lesson here is that sometimes people cancel not because they have to but because they just don't feel like coming or want to do something else.

What if they don't make a decision to book a consultation?

It does happen where we get a lead either through Facebook or via phone call that does not book a consultation. Most businesses just let these people fall out of their universe. Not us and hopefully, now, not you.

When we get a lead, they are put on a very sophisticated lead sheet. It tracks when they contacted us, what they are interested in and all of their contact information.

We have a structured follow-up process for these people and if we do not book them for a consultation after about 6 attempts, we move them to lost leads list and our general email newsletter list. The email list will continue to educate them and also give them many more opportunities to re-engage with us. As far as direct contact, we give them some breathing room but mark my words, we will be back.

Shake the trees

We have a term we use at GFP called shake the trees. The purpose is to reach out to older leads that were unconverted.

We do this when we have not met our consultation goal for that week or our leads are slow and we foresee it being harder to meet our consult goals.

Having the lost lead list is key here. Karen just smiles and dials.

Role Playing

I cannot stress enough how important making this process better truly is.

For a very long time I never did any training to improve the lead conversion process.

Once I understood how truly important this process is, we started working hard to make it better.

One of the reasons a script is so important is because you can see what is actually working.

If your people just do whatever they want, and everyone does it in their own way, it's going to be hard to pinpoint what they are actually doing to make it successful or unsuccessful.

So, step one is building the foundation (the script).

Step 2 is practicing in an environment where immediate feedback is given.

Have you ever been on a call where a recording came on saying "this call may be monitored for quality assurance"?

They are recording their calls to be able to either get rid of bad performers or use it for training purposes.

You need to do some version of this, too.

Role playing is not easy because people will need to accept constructive criticism. Some people are better at it than others, so it's important to know how to give people feedback that will be productive.

I can yell and scream at our CEO, Big Tom, all day long. He'll be fine and, honestly, will probably improve.

If I did that with other members of our team, they would melt like a candle. You must know who you're working with and treat them accordingly.

This is not an easy thing for people to do. They know they are being evaluated so they may get nervous and actually get worse. Press on.

Continually reassure them this is to help them do their job better so the business can accomplish its vision.

I cannot stress enough that the people doing this job must know the importance and that's it too important to be left for chance.

Having a weekly meeting and practicing this stuff on a regular basis will quickly get you to a fairly rare category – not everyone is willing to put in the time.

Also, the bigger you get and more people you have fielding incoming leads, the more this needs to be trained.

Secret shopping

I did this recently with one of my mastermind members.

He was having trouble getting leads to come in for a consult, so I called his gym and pretended to be looking for training.

One of the mistakes his employee made was going deep into what they did, something I teach people NOT to do. She talked about all their different classes and even started talking about very specific pieces of equipment like versa climbers and ski ergs.

I knew what they were, but most normal people would not. Starting people off confused is a big mistake. She also mostly hit on features but left out the benefits, a very important concept that's something we will cover later in this book.

I found many holes in his admin's delivery and was able to give him many things for her to work on.

Setting the goals

Having a goal for the amount of consultations you want to book is probably the most underused strategy in the fitness business.

We look to convert, on average, 50% of our leads to come in for a consultation. Note that referral type leads will be higher and cold traffic like Facebook and Google ads will be lower.

So, for every 10 calls we get, 5 should schedule and attend the consultation.

Making your team aware of this number is how to actually achieve it effectively.

I went out and purchased 10 life preserver magnets and told our team to put up a magnet every time we booked a consultation.

This served a few purposes:

1. There was a visual of success or failure.

As the week went on and we were not yet at our goal, I found people were flipping over rocks to hit it. They were following up more times, going back to the previous month's lost leads and were even calling old members to come back, just to hit that goal of 10 consultations booked.

2. It provided a visual that made this a very important job.

The life preserver signified that every consultation was a life saved. They were doing their part in helping that person transform their life by booking that consultation. This pushes people to get the job done.

CHAPTER 5:
HOW TO HOLD AN INCREDIBLE CONSULTATION

I'll soon be taking the stage at the Perform Better Conference in Providence, Rhode Island. My topic is titled the most important hour in fitness. That's the consultation.

Here's why it's the most important hour in fitness.

It's most important for them *and* most important for you.

It's most important for them because this meeting sets the tone for an experience that will be different. An experience that they've never had before, where they will feel hope that this is a place that's going to transform their life.

Its most important for you because if this meeting does not go well, there is good chance they won't stay and an opportunity to change a life and add profit to your bottom line has been lost.

First impressions are crucial, and the consultation process is the first in-person experience they have with you. It must be perfect.

Step 1: Build Rapport

I recently visited a local deli in my town. It was my first time there and there was some confusion about where to go to order my sandwich. I'm not a small guy so I don't think they missed me, but I was kind of pacing back and

48

forth trying to figure out this maze of getting a sandwich.

I finally found the right place and some rude kid yells "next!" There were about 100 things on the menu so it took me a while to order. He took my order, which was put on a pile for someone else to get to. I waited for close to 15 minutes and they had not even started my sandwich. They were not even busy (shocker). I was boiling. I cancelled my order and left the place and never went back.

Building rapport does not start when you sit down with people and start asking them questions.

Building rapport starts when they pull up to the parking lot. Every little thing that happens after they get out of their car is an opportunity to either build or lose their trust.

When I had my first facility, I did a poor job of this.

We used to keep garbage in the back of the parking lot. Many times, the wind would act up and blow boxes and packing popcorn all over the lot.

I was not great at clean up and neither were my coaches. It went so far as a good client coming up to me and saying "Vince, you need keep your parking lot cleaner. If I'm paying $500/month for gym membership I don't want to pull up to a tornado of garbage." It hurt to hear it, but he was 100% right.

Keeping the outside of your building clean is a sign you care enough about your business and your members to keep a clean area.
"Should someone be at the front desk?"

I get asked this all the time from rookie gym owners that want to hire an admin.

People that do not know how to manage people will tell this gym owner to hire a virtual assistant that works off-site.

They'll say employees are a headache. In some instances they are correct, but an inability to manage people is big reason why many gym owners struggle so much after a little initial success.

I view this as a huge mistake.

An administrative assistant can start the rapport building process by being the first nice, friendly face clients see when they walk into your gym.

Know They're Coming

A monster step in building rapport is when you demonstrate that you know people are coming.

An example here is a little chalkboard we put on our front desk. It shows the names of the people that will be coming to GFP for the first time.

They walk in and their first experience is seeing their name on the board and having a nice friendly face greet them by name as well.

It's the ultimate rapport builder.

The Consultation Room

In my first facility, I made some very big mistakes.

One of the biggest was not doing a great job using my office for a consultation room. Instead, I simply did consults in my office.

The difference between the two is that my office was also my locker. I had sweaty clothes in the bottom drawers, Tupperware containers all around, 3-week-old shaker bottles and crappy chairs that the landlord gave me when we signed a lease.

I can remember many times walking a client into my office, having them sit down and then cleaning the shakers, papers and Tupperware containers off the desk. It was because I was so busy running from one thing to the next that I never slowed down enough to prepare the environment of the consultations room.

Now, in our new facility we have a 10x10 office that is only used for consultations.

Here is what's inside that office and why it's important.

Round tables: When you sit across a desk it reminds people of an old school sales environment where you are going to twist their arm and lock them into a 3-year membership. Round tables imply that you are going to work *with* them. Sitting next to them and going over all the things they are going to do to get results makes them feel more like this is collaborative process, not a sales pitch. Ditch the desks and put round tables in – they're a lot cheaper, too

If you only have one office in your facility, my advice is

to build it as a consultation room first and your office second. In my new gym I have my own office, but it is structured so it can be a consultation room if we had 2 consultations at the same time.

I keep everything I need in my backpack and we have a small filing cabinet that can hold any papers I need, but that's pretty much it.

Testimonials on the Walls

We have our walls filled with our happy, satisfied members. We make sure when they sit down they face the wall that holds all the pictures so the entire time they are looking at social proof that what we do works.

For a template we use to put Client Testimonials on the wall visit www.ultimategymguide.com.

Books

One of the most important things you can do early in the rapport-building process is to demonstrate that you are an expert.

Writing a book, no matter if anyone ever bought a single copy, shows a level of expertise and professionalism that helps you stand out from your competition. We have produced 5 books as a company and they are all proudly displayed on a strategically-placed shelf in the consultation room.

Supplements

We will unpack how we profit from supplements in a later chapter, but the supplements we sell are also displayed in the consultation room. We believe that supplements should be part of a well-rounded fitness program and are not shy about building supplements into clients' ideal health and fitness program. It's not a hard sell. Rather, it's just built into what is best for them and their results.

Asking How They Got to You

When we sit down with them in our highly thought-out selling environment, we always ask leads about how they got to us.

This usually brings up the conversation about the specific person that referred them, which puts them at ease.

That helps put at ease issues they may be nervous about and goes to a topic where we and the client have a common friend.

This also sets the tone for referral conversations.

We tell them that most of our members come from referrals and we're going to be taking great care of the friend that sent them to us.

This implies that the people that train at your gym tell their friends about you.

You're simply planting a seed – and it needs to be planted, every time.

Find the goal

Two years ago, I sat in my office with an incredible woman.

Her name was Cathy Balsamo and she was just selected to participate in our sweepstakes challenge.

This was a program where we advertised we were giving away 6 free weeks of training at our gym.

We had people fill a very lengthy application and then selected the 4 most qualified people to participate, and Cathy was one of our winners.

For more info on the sweepstakes, and trust me you want this as its been the most successful marketing event we've ever done, you can read about it in my first book the Ultimate Guide to Marketing Your Gym, you can get it here, www.ultimategymguide.com

Cathy had a long history of going on different diets but had never joined a gym. She was a very happy person and a center of influence in our community.

But she had health issues. She was on several medications, was overweight and was on her way down a bad road with her health.

In our first meeting I started to ask her what she wanted to accomplish.

She said the normal things like "I need to get off these meds and lose weight." I knew that was not enough.

Having a goal of losing weight was not going to make a massive change in her life.

I started to ask her why she wanted to lose weight.

She started to get a little uncomfortable. She was not used to anyone asking her a question like that.

It was a simple question: why?

She started to talk about her kids. How she never wanted her kids to be like her. She wanted them to live a long and healthy life.

As she is talking this out she starts to realize that she not only needs to do this to lose weight, get off meds and get healthy, but she needs to do this to be a role model for her family.

That was a moment that changed her life.

2 ½ years later I am proud to report that Cathy has lost close to 90 pounds and has been that role model for her family.

But then something even more amazing happened.

She was not only a role model for her family, she became the role model for an entire community.

Since Cathy had such a following, people were really tuned in to her progress during the sweepstakes.

They started to see her success from the videos we were putting out on a weekly basis.

It created a massive wave of people that became interested in her and, by default, interested in us.

She motivated countless women to come and start training at GFP but also motivated countless more to just get healthy on their own.

This one woman simply took over an entire community and changed a ton of lives.

It all started with a conversation.

A question.

A question that uncovered the true reason why she needed to get her life back and the thing that still keeps her going 2 ½ years later.

Most sales processes involve a customer coming in to a store, the owner of the store telling them about the features of the product or service and then a sale possibly taking place.

The missing link in most sales experiences is asking the right questions.

There is a secret you need to know.

People do not care about you.

They don't care about your training philosophy, your equipment, your certifications or your training programs.

They about themselves.

They care about their results.

They want someone to listen.

The biggest role of a great sales person.

Ask the right questions and listen for the best answers.

To get your mitts on the questions we ask in the consultation, visit www.ultimategymguide.com/salesbook

Step 3: Build the Value

Once you establish rapport and make it clear you are interested in them and what they want to accomplish, the next step is to start making the connection between what they want and what you do.

There is a stark difference between these two things

1. An MP3 player that stores 1 GB.

2. 1,000 songs in your pocket.

The first one is a feature of an iPod.

The second is a benefit of an iPod.

People need to hear features but what will move them closer to a sale are the benefits that what you do can bring them.

Let's take a high-intensity interval-training class that you may be describing to a potential member as an example.

You start to talk about how you use Kettlebells, ropes, ski Ergs and rowers. To you, that stuff is cool. But it's very possible they may not know what the heck any of these things even are.

The key is to connect them to the benefit of the features the equipment provides.

A phrase you can use is "SO YOU CAN."

The formula goes like this:

"We use various types of equipment in our fat blast so

you can boost your metabolism and burn fat for the entire rest of the day."

To them, boosting metabolism is probably something they know about and they definitely know they want to burn fat.

Stopping at the features is a massive mistake many gym owners make. Connect them to the benefits of what you do.

This is also a time to utilize tools like the functional movement screen.

I have been using the FMS for close to 15 years and every client that has trained in my gym for the past 10 years has been screened.

If you train adults, many of them will come in with pre-existing injuries like shoulder, knee or back issues.

This is par for the course for the adult fitness market and the successful gyms are the ones that can train people safely despite these issues.

A tool like the FMS will communicate to the member that you care about their well-being. It differentiates you from other places that may just throw them into the fire and will also make you sound smart, which will build further trust.

It also gives you an opportunity to show the value of individuation and that you will focus on their personal needs.

An example could be if they had a shoulder issue. The FMS can clearly show there could be a risk for injury if they do things like excessive overhead pressing on a bad wing.

You build the value by explaining that because of this discovery in the consultation, we will avoid any overhead work in the short term to make sure they are staying healthy.

You assure them that they will still get the best possible workout but that you'll just work around the shoulder.

People appreciate this more than you could imagine.

It's kind of like showing up at a restaurant you've been before and they know, without being prompted, that you have an allergy to dairy. It's just a really nice feeling to know people care about your well-being.

Another key factor in the consultation is talking to them about their nutrition. Most people in the adult fitness market want to lose weight. The earlier you help them lose weight, the more likely they will be to sign up at your gym.

It's not the only thing that matters, but it's definitely important – if, in fact, it's important to them.

Think of the woman that has been struggling to lose weight for years.

You tell her to stop eating carbs for breakfast and she drops body fat in the first week.

It seems basic to you but to them this early success is a game changer and could be a major deciding factor in them signing up.

Asking about their nutrition and offering some simple basic habits that will be easy to implement but still get them results is a key factor in building the value of what you do.

To take it a step further, you telling them about how you not only will help them with what to eat but also hold them accountable via regular meetings or check-ins further starts to connect what they want with what you do.

Step 4: Create the Prescription

When I was participating in the Goldman Sachs 10,000 Small Business Program I had a business advisor named Rod Dauphin.

Rod knew his shit and was a former college football player like me, so I had a ton of respect for him.

One day we were working on my growth plan and I started talking a lot. I started to try to take over the conversation as I was just getting into what we were doing.

Rod look at me dead in the eyes, held up his hand and said these words:

"Vince, (long pause) I'm going to control the conversation now."

It was as if he hit me with a taser.

I froze.

No one ever said anything like that to me, but from then on, I listened a lot more to what Rod was saying and implemented it.

Rod established control and it made me respect and listen to him even more.

Many gyms allow the prospect to control the buying process.

They allow people to come in and tell them what they want to do.

An example is a client coming in and saying, "I want to train with kettlebells and I want to do it 7 days a week because that's what I read in women's health magazine," and they do it.

This will never earn their respect for long.

People want to be told what to do, but many do not give them the chance to do it.

If you establish what needs to be done in a respectful, helpful way, people will follow you.

When they do, they trust you more, their results will be better and everyone will win.

Here's an example using the tale of 2 massage therapists.

The first therapist asks me what areas I want to work on today. I tell her my back and legs. She does it.

The second therapists asks what I want to accomplish. I tell her I want to get rid of my low back pain. She confidently tells me that the main causes of back pain usually stem from tight hips and a tight thoracic spine, so she will focus on those areas.

I trust the second therapist much more because she was in charge and took control.

If you remember back to the earlier chapter about clarity, success in sales is being able to help people wade through the muck of information and develop a clear, simple, easy strategy for success.

We use something called a health road map to help people with this.

It outlines everything they need to do for their health on one page.

This includes their goals, their why, their food, their fitness, their accountability and even their supplement needs – all summarized on one sheet of paper.

They leave our consultations with everything they need to do on one simple, easy-to-read page.

It's been a game changer for our business and has been a tool adopted by many of our mastermind members.

The health road map puts you in a different category than everyone else because you are setting the tone for what needs to be done.

Instead of trying to explain it all here, go to this link and check out a video I made that unpacks the health road map in detail. Visit www.ultimategymguide.com to get it.

CHAPTER 6:
THE TRIAL MEMBERSHIP

There is an amazing burger place on the west coast called In and Out Burger.

No matter what time you go to this place there is always a massive line and people gladly wait on it.

In and Out has the following things on their menu:

- Burgers
- Fries
- Shakes

That's it.

No chicken sandwich, no fish filet, no breakfast sandwiches. They don't even serve coffee.

In a world where everyone is trying to be all things to all people, these guys just keep crushing it by doing a few things really well.

But the other thing that makes this so effective is that there so little decision fatigue.

When I go to a Jersey Diner and there are 211 different omelets I can choose from, it just makes me frustrated.

Too many gyms have so many different services and price options that it makes it hard for people to make a buying decision.

I use a slide in one of my sales presentations that shows

one gym's price sheet with 36 different options to choose from.

There is a reason why people offer so many options, and it's usually fear of loss.

They feel like if they don't have something for everyone, they will lose people

Most training gyms I work with charge $200-500 per month for a gym membership.

Asking for that kind of money up front is like asking to get married on the first date, it usually does not end well.

The key is making it as easy as possible for people to get started.

There is no easier way than just selling one option that is so enticing it's almost impossible for them to say no.

We do this with a trial membership.

The trial membership is short-term, lower-priced test drive of your gym.

Typically, a 30-day trial is the most common, but I have seen 6-week, 15-day and even 7-day trial periods work just fine.

All of your marketing should be designed to drive people to eventually buy your trial membership. It should be the only way into your door.

We typically always charge for this and the cost has ranged from $21-$499 depending on the length and what is included.

I am not a huge fan of free trials for high-value, long-term membership, but again, everything is worth a test as this may be the thing that is right for your gym.

What to Give During the Trial

I have a friend that goes to the grocery store and specifically looks for packages of lunch meat that have this huge orange sticker on it that says:

"Half-price, almost expired."

I don't know about you, but lunch meat is shady as it is, waiting until it's almost expired just seems gross to me.

Many people do this for their trial membership.

Since they are charging less money because it's an intro offer, they give people less.

Let's take a moment and pretend you decided to test drive a BMW.

They don't bring around the stripped beamer that has the factory wheels and no bells and whistles, do they?

Nope, they bring around the fully-loaded option with the sunroof, heated leather seats, chrome wheels and turbo engine.

When you get into that car and experience all that stuff, you want it, even if you need to pay a little more.

Funneling people into a test drive for your gym might be one of the most important things to do to make serious money in the long term.
Selling a lower cost trial membership enables them to

experience what you do before you ask for a long-term commitment.

The trial needs to be an experience.

It needs to showcase what you do to drive people to the highest possible membership they can afford.

If you have additional services like interval training classes, yoga sessions, stretching services, Pilates, nutrition, etc., it all should be included in the trial so they can experience everything you do.

If you let them experience the 7-series package, they will probably buy it.

If you let them experience the 3-series package, they will probably buy it.

I know I want to sell many more 7-series packages.

Put people in the best position to buy your highest value offering by giving that to them during their trial.

Win them during the trial.

The trial membership all comes down to getting people to say:

"This is place for me, I've never experienced anything like this before."

How often you follow-up, how quickly you remember their name, how quickly you get them results and how you can make them feel like they are not a number, but rather an important member of your community, are all keys to making this happen.

We have a very specific follow-up process we use during the trial that's a combination of text messages, emails and phone calls. To take a peek visit www. ultimategymguide.com.

The Final Meeting: Ringing the Register

If all the stuff leading to this point is done well, this step of the process requires the least amount of skill.

Most people put all their stock into handling objections and miss the point that the sales process simply needs to be about earning trust.

By this point, the person has usually made up their mind as to a yes or no. It's about putting them into the right place to buy as well as the place that keeps the average value per member at your goal.

Important: this meeting needs to be scheduled at the initial consultation and it should be clearly explained that this is where they will be asked to make a decision.

This meeting normally starts with the question:

"What can you tell me about your experience?"

This gets them talking and will highlight what things they valued most from their time with you.

You'd be shocked at how many people say the most valuable thing was that my team remembered their name, or that it was nice having an appointment where I showed up and told them what to do.

It's best to have options for them to choose from, almost

as if you are placing them in the right program.

If you want to position yourself as an authority, showing up to that meeting with options as to what is best for them makes people feel like you have a handle on their success.

Present the 2-3 options you feel are best fit.

Unpack the options highlighting what's included and their various benefits.

Then ask this simple question:

"Which one of these works best for you?"

Then, take a roll of duct tape and tape your mouth shut. ☺

It's old school sales stuff but it truly works. Sit there in silence and even when it gets uncomfortable, don't talk first.

Handling Objections

With all of that being said, there will be times where people have objections and it's important to be prepared.

The real objection handling should be done throughout the entire sales process.

Here are some common objections with some responses.

1. If they say it's too expensive: Just curious about that, too expensive compared to what?

2. If they need to think about it: Follow up question: tell me a little more, what is it you want to think over?

3. If they want to ask their spouse: Great! Let's set up a time for the 3 of us to sit down and talk.

4. If they want a lower option: Try to start them on higher option and let them know they can change it after a few months.

5. If they're very hesitant about a 12-month commitment: No problem, I'll give you a 30 day out. If after 30 days you feel this is not for you, we'll part as friends. They still should sign a 12-month contract here.

6. If they don't want to start yet: Get them to sign the contract and date the contract for the future date they want to start. Let them know if they're around, they can pop in and train at no cost.

If they make it clear they are interested but they cannot make a decision that day, here's what you need to do:

Ask them when they would be able to make a decision. Schedule a meeting or a phone call for that time. Make it an appointment. The more you leave open ended the less chance for a conversion at this point.

Point of Sale Referral

Once a client commits to a contract, they are the most excited and will be in the best frame of mind to refer us a new member.

Think about when you buy a car. Let's say you got a Honda Pilot. For a while, every time you see another Honda Pilot it will become more important to you and be front and center in your mind.

It's a part of your brain called the reticular activating system.

When you make big decisions like purchasing a car or a gym membership, this part of your brain lights up and you are more likely to tell others about it.

Taking advantage of this time is essential to generating high-quality referrals.

Here's what to say:

We'd love to celebrate your new membership with the great act of giving.

I'd like to offer you a 30-day trial membership for free to give to a friend.

Show them a physical card that they can give to a friend

We love black metal business cards and I believe they are superior to most other options, but they can be costly. So if you're just starting out, maybe just make them yourself.

The important questions you need to ask:

Who would you like to give this to?

This implies they need to think of a very specific person and will usually deliver better results than just giving them the card on its own.

This needs to be baked into your system.

This needs to be done 100% of the time and should never ever not be done.

It's the lowest hanging fruit you could possibly imagine.

We also keep a pretty structured follow up system for this, too.

We track who took a black metal card, whether they gave us a name, if we are waiting to hear back from them about giving us an introduction and if that person came in.

To check out a spreadsheet we use to track all of this visit www.ultimategymguide.com

CHAPTER 7:
PRICING, THE REAL SECRET TO MAKING MONEY

I almost killed my wife.

Our first daughter's first birthday was a big deal.

We had a party and invited a ton of people, it was a great time.

Then, Vanessa brought out the cake.

The cake was magnificent – it looked like art and I almost felt bad about cutting into it.

Everyone was commenting about how nice the cake was.

While we were cleaning up I told Vanessa how the party was great, and the cake was amazing.

She quietly smiled.

I asked her where she got the cake.

She faintly mentioned some obscure bakery that was an hour away from us I had never heard of.

I kept on cleaning.

On the car ride home, I could not stop thinking about that cake.

I turned to Vanessa and asked her how much the cake was.

She turned beat red and said "well, I'm not totally sure, I'll have to check the receipt."

I asked her again, with a little more gusto.

"How much was that (insert expletive) cake? (Catching myself) Honey?"

I knew it was going to be a whopper.

It turns out the cake was $379!!

I almost jumped out of the moving car.

To me, a $4 box of Betty Crocker Cake mix and a $2 pack of frosting would have been perfect.

But for my wife, this was our first daughter's first birthday, an event that would never happen again.

The cake, while crazy to me, made perfect sense to her because of the significance of the event.

Everyone has their thing.

I won't bat an eye at a $200 massage because of how much I value my health and managing my stress.

Some people pay $2,000 a year at Starbucks. I think that's ludicrous because their coffee is garbage (I'm a bit of a coffee snob).

Some pay $500 per hour to get a private tour guide at Disney.

In terms of how much you charge for your services:

What you consider value does not matter.

The only thing that matters with pricing is what your members consider value.

Most of our issues with pricing start with our own beliefs:

"People project their own past and present relationship with money and what they will spend for things onto their customers."- Dan Kennedy

The most money I ever made before I became a gym owner was $37,000 a year.

The thought of me spending $500 for a gym membership was not even a consideration.

But to the doctors, lawyers and businessmen that train at my gym, $500 a month to keep their energy up, stress down and have someone tell them what to do when they go arrive is a no-brainer.

One of most critical factors that will make you more money as a gym owner is having the right pricing structure.

Your prices being too low or your profitability being poor is a gateway to an unhappy career as a gym owner. I happen to believe that most training gyms are priced too low.

How Much Should You Charge

Most people do not set themselves up to have a gym that makes good money because they are priced too low or too high.

I see gym owners offering only one very low-priced option, which makes it hard to make money because you're playing a volume game.

I also see them offering only 1-1 training at $80 bucks a session.

I don't think they realize that when you break this out over a month you're asking people to pay close to $1000 a month for personal training. Most people cannot afford that long term.

How much to charge depends on many factors, but the big mistake is looking at what the guy down the street is charging and either going a little higher or lower.

Your location must also be considered.

You probably will not be able to charge New York City prices in a rural area of Michigan that has an average household income of $25,000.

Here are a few guidelines:

1. How much money do you want to make?

At the end of the day, you control how much to charge. There is no governing body that restricts you from charging what you want.

This is where a concept called price elasticity becomes important.

Price elasticity is the degree to which you can stretch your prices relative to your competition.

The first and best way to be able to stretch your prices,

i.e. to charge more money, than your competition is to offer something completely different.

The more you are like other gyms, the more people will compare your price to the person down the street.

The more unique you are, the less they will see the comparison and the more you can charge.

2. What is your base operating expense?

Something else to determine is exactly how much it costs you to operate your facility per hour.

This is as simple as taking all of your fixed expenses and dividing that number by the number of potential hours you are open.

If it costs $100 per hour to simply run your facility between rent, utilities, insurance, etc., then you need to charge enough money to earn more than that.

If you only charge $20 per session and you allow 5 people in the session, based on the 100 per hour run rate you will essentially be losing money.

3. What services you are offering

How much to charge depends largely on the services you are offering. Here is the simplest way I can break this down. The services I see most often at personal training gyms are:

- Large group (20-40 people) $10-20/session
- Small Group Personal Training (2-4 People) $30-60/ session
- $80-120/session

There are some that run a program that has 6-15 people, but I have not seen that to be very successful as its kind of in the middle. It's usually a hybrid of large and small groups, but is normally priced closer to large group versus small.

The people I usually coach that run this model usually end up making this their large group option and then add a higher priced small group.

That being said, this option may be a great case for lower-income areas where higher prices may be tougher to get.

"It's too expensive!"

I often hear gym owners say clients claim their services are too expensive, and that's why they go elsewhere.

Usually when people say it's too expensive, it's because the value of the service provided to that specific person did not match the investment.

There are some people that truly cannot afford it – that's a given.

However, in my experience the "too expensive" people are usually the same people that got poor results, did not gel with the culture or just had too much going on in their life to sign up.

The key is being good enough at sales to match the value to the person with the investment.

This is why the consultation is so important. It gives you the opportunity to understand what they value and then match that value with your right program.

This is a reason why I love small group personal training.

There's probably no one in your area doing it well. They either do 1-1, large groups or some bastardized version of a small group that has 8-12 people in it.

A true small group personal training session where you can deliver an experience and results comparable to 1-1 is about 2-4 people.

When you can deliver the same results and experience, charge half as much and still make double the money, you're on to something.

Much more on this later.

Good Better Best

One of my favorite TV shows is The Profit on CNBC. It stars an investor named Marcus Lemonis who goes into struggling businesses and turns them around.

He was working with a company that made drums for musicians.

The guys were struggling because they only sold one product: drum set that cost about $2,000.

Marcus jumped in and created a new pricing structure for them using a pricing strategy called good, better, best.

He kept the $2,000 set but added a lower-priced drum for beginners for $800.

He also created another option for $8,000 for an experienced professional drummer.

They now opened themselves up to a much wider array of drummers but still focused on their core product, making drums.

Let's look at the good, better, best strategy using a BMW example again.

- The 3-series starts at $35,000.

- The 5-series starts at $52,000.

- The 7-series starts at $83,000.

They are all great cars from a great manufacturer, but they attract a different kind of customer.

If a person walks into the BMW dealership and is looking to spend $20 thousand for a new car, they probably should have gone to the Ford dealer.

Having a layered pricing structure allows you to have options for multiple price points within your target market.

If you only sold $199 per month group fitness, the 50-year-old doctor that wants more attention and coaching might not have a place at your gym.

Conversely, the 40-year-old mom that wants to do classes and be part of a large group and community may not fit if you only sold small group training for $500 per month.

Being able to serve both of these people gives you a larger slice of the pie but still allows you to stay in a focused target market.

The Layered Pricing Structure

This is pretty much the secret sauce that Tom Plummer has taught me and many of the top gym owners in America.

Unpacking this is beyond the scope of this book, but contact me to learn more and I'll get on the phone and give you pretty much everything you need to know.

Just shoot me an email at Vince@gabrielefitness.com and put layered pricing in the subject!

The $10,000 dress

Vera Wang is a clothing designer that actually sells a $10,000 dress that you can only buy their store.

They also sell a $99 scarf that you can buy at local discount stores like Target.

The people that see the $99 scarf but don't know about the $10 thousand dress may turn their nose at the scarf.

But the people that know about the $10 thousand dress will look at the scarf as a steal.

Having an option whose sole purpose is to make your regular prices look small is a sound business decision.

We have an option on our price sheet in a big red box that says "super-secret training program, $1,999 per month."

No one has ever bought it, but it sure makes our premium option of $499 look pretty small.

When people ask what that is, and many people do, we

usually just tell them that it's not necessary for them and point them to the option that's the best fit.

It also builds trust as we're telling them NOT to buy something very expensive.

Small Group Versus 1-1 pricing

If you're still considering choosing 1-1 over small group personal training, check out this math.

Four people at $50 is $200 per hour. If the people in this session came 8x/month, they would pay $400/month.

One person at $100 is, well, $100 per hour. If the person came 8x/month they would pay $800/month.

Asking someone to pay $800/month for an extended period of time in any market is a tall order.

Not to mention that, as you can see, your hourly intake is double, and you can pay the trainer the same amount either way, so your profitability is through the roof.

So, they pay less and you make more – a lot more. It seems like a no-brainer to me.

If you really want a simple formula for pricing small group personal training, you can use this one I got from Rick Mayo. Find out what the average rate is for a 30-minute 1-1 session and charge that for small group. It's not perfect, but it's pretty simple and will probably get you pretty close to where you want to be.

*Want to hear a ton more about
small group personal training?
Check out this podcast episode we did that
unpacks everything we know about it.*

*http://www.vincegabriele.com/podcast-episode-013-
the-four-secrets-of-small-group-personal-training/*

Should you ever sell 1-1?

No!

Ok, I'm just kidding.

Here are some situations where 1-1 may be a good idea:
- The client has injuries.
- The client has health history issues.
- The client is older than your normal members.

This client may need lots of attention and you might feel like you'd be putting them at risk even in a small group. The real consideration that needs to be made, then, is if they are actually a fit for your gym.

There are several cases we take on ONLY if they agree to 1-1 for a pretty high hourly rate and for an agreed-upon short-term time-frame where they then would go into our small group.

CHAPTER 8:
MORE MONEY PER MEMBER

One of the MOST important numbers you could possibly track is your gym's average monthly value per member.

If you do not know this number, please figure it out as soon as possible.

If you spend a large portion your time trying to drive up the average monthly value of each member, then that will make your business very successful.

Several factors matter here, but the most important is that your monthly membership prices are priced properly (as we've discussed earlier).

Getting the right amount of money for your membership often comes down to your own self-confidence.

The better your confidence, the more you will be willing to charge. If you want to make more money, you'll probably need to start from within.

So, the right pricing structure is #1 and we covered that in detail already.

Here are a few other ways to get more money per member after you've established a profitable membership structure.

Creating Opportunities for Membership Upgrades

This morning I am up early getting ready for a big day in my kids' lives. My 5 and 6-year-old daughters have been working very hard all week getting ready for their first lemonade stand.

They were inspired by a children's book I read to them by Andy Frisella called The Fantastic Fruit Stand.

We had a team meeting, took a trip to BJs, made signs, tasted a ton of lemonade and we're finally ready to launch.

This has given me a great opportunity to teach them about business, money, hard work and discipline.

One of the things I've talked to them about is how to ask for the sale.

The question we've been practicing is not "how can I help you?"

The question we've been practicing is "how many glasses of lemonade would you like?"

This will get people thinking about who else they may want to buy a lemonade for and, most likely, if they planned on one glass, this question will increase the possibility of a second glass purchased, and possibly even a third or fourth.

Once they order lemonade, the follow up questions is:

"Would you like any fruit or water with your lemonade?"

There is a reason why every time you go to Panera, they,

like clockwork, ask if you would like a cookie with your order.

The amount of money Panera makes on upsells must be gaudy.

The key thing with all of this is to simply ask.

We recently ran a 6-week challenge where our members paid $97 to enter. With their entry, they received a membership upgrade.

As mentioned earlier, we use a layered pricing structure.

Whatever membership they were on, they all got one level above where they were, and the value was about $100/ month or more.

During the challenge, we emailed participants and asked if they were interested in speaking to us about continuing with the upgraded membership.

The key word here is "upgrade." If you've ever been lucky enough to have gone from coach to first class on an airplane, you were upgraded to first class.

Asking them if they would like to speak with us about the upgrade is called getting permission to sell.

We are asking for their permission to sell them something and, when they agree, they become very qualified to make this purchase.

Sending them an email asking if they want to do it or not is less work but would not have been as effective.

Instead, we brought them in for a meeting and talked

about the benefits of the upgraded membership and offered a free gift if they signed up before the challenge ended.

We had 10 people take us up on the upgrade. This equated to $1,000 of monthly recurring revenue without adding another client and with a very minimal increase in expenses.

In order to take advantage of this you need a tiered pricing structure. Once that's in place, all you need to do is ask your clients if they want to upgrade their membership.

Their results will improve and so will your profits.

Supplements

Many gym owners say they don't sell supplements, and I think this is silly.

This is a billion-dollar industry for a reason and not capitalizing on it is simply not smart.

The reality is this: I am close to positive that you take supplements. Why don't you want to give your clients that same opportunity while also ensuring they get their supplements from a reputable source?

Your clients are going to take supplements. If they don't know the difference between garbage and the good stuff, they will take the garbage you can buy from CVS or Walgreens.

Supplements are not all created equal and that is the key to making money from them at your gym. Sell a high-quality product and educate your members about why they're the better option.

You most likely have access to good quality supplements and sell them at a higher price than the garbage at CVS, but it's justified because they trust you. I recommend finding a brand you can sell that you cannot buy anywhere else.

If you sell the same stuff they can buy on Amazon for cheaper, they probably will catch on and just get it shipped to their home.

The math on this is simple.

If you get 100 members purchasing supplements on a monthly basis for roughly $50/month, that is $5,000 in monthly revenue at a really nice margin.

You make more money per member and they get a high-quality product that makes them healthier. It's a win/win.

What you sell depends upon your market.

If you serve the 40-60-year-old fitness client looking to live longer and stay in shape, then the following will probably be sufficient:

- Magnesium
- Vitamin D
- Fish Oil
- Multivitamin
- Protein Powder
- Greens Powder

If you want to add more from a performance standpoint, adding things like BCAA, glutamine, and creatine may be an option.

Sell Water, Bars and Ready to Drink Shakes

If you get a fridge and fill it up with water and ready-to-drink shakes, people will definitely buy them.

You won't see a huge bang in revenue, but it adds up over time and it takes little effort. It's also an added value to your members to have this stuff available.

We sell Fiji water, RX bars and Orgain ready-to-drink shakes at GFP.

My rule for pricing on supplements is this: you buy for $20 and sell for $40. If the item is too expensive to sell at this markup, I don't sell it.

There are some people that have had success with juice bars in their gyms but I have not seen enough of them to recommend if this is a viable opportunity.

Selling Gear

One of the guys that speak with me on the Perform Better Tour is Martin Rooney, the founder of Training for Warriors (TFW).

To say Martin has a big following is a monstrous understatement. There are dozens of people walking around the conference proudly wearing their black-and-yellow TFW t-shirts.

It's like Martin has this mini army walking around flying his flag.

Building a community is one of the most impactful things you can do to have a successful gym. When people wear clothing with your name on it, they are making a statement.

A statement that they have bought into your mission. If someone wears your shirt every time they workout, what are the chances they are going to leave? Probably small.

Many people think that wearing the shirts is advertising, and in a way, it is.
But something more powerful happens that drives the all-important referral conversations.

It's called omnipresence.

When people are surrounded by your brand, you are always on their mind. When you are always on their mind, their likelihood to refer to you a great new member is very high.

I will be diving deep in referral-based marketing in another volume of the Ultimate Guide Series, so stay tuned.

So, what should you sell?

T-shirts are an obvious choice because they will get worn the most. Don't do what I did and go cheap for many years.

I loved the old school heavy cotton t-shirts and also liked them because they were cheap, big mistake.

If you don't make a ton of money on your gear it's not the end of the world.

Get cool stuff that people will actually want to wear, not just because it looks good but because they like the feel of the material and it doesn't feel like a free t-shirt they got at a 5 K race.

Get lots of different versions, colors and themes.

We have printed close to 50 different styles of T-shirts in our 10-year existence.

Think of an alternative logo to your gym name, too. We used a great version for a long time called GFPSTRONG that a ton of people bought into.

Selling women's tank tops is also a great call as they normally do not want to wear the men's style t-shirts.

Hooded sweatshirts are another great seller, but I guess if you live in places like San Diego you won't sell as much.

For gear like shirts and sweatshirts, we just mark it up a little differently than supplements because we do not want the cost to demotivate people to buy.

We want them walking around flying our flag.

Equipment

Selling things like foam rollers, massage sticks and bands gives your clients something to work on at home and gives you another revenue stream.

This most likely is not a big one, but if you sell, people will buy. We get everything from *www.performbetter.com*.

CHAPTER 9:
GETTING OLD MEMBERS BACK AND SAVING THE ONES YOU HAVE

I was doing yoga with my wife in our living room and had an epiphany.

I always hate doing yoga but feel amazing when I'm done.

I had recently joined a yoga studio and was doing 1-2 classes a week.

My body felt great.

I slowly stopped going, so I cancelled it.

I turned to my wife during savasana (yes, the thing where you're just supposed to relax and not talk) and said this.

"You know, if that yoga studio just called to ask me to come back, I would."

If you're running a sound operation, most people leave because of something to do with them, not you.

In my case, I just got busy and stopped going. I loved the classes, but certainly was not going to pay for it if I was not using it.

There's always a great chance people will come back.

In my 11 years of running a gym, I've had tons of people come back after they terminated their membership.

Some after a few months, others after a few years.

We actually had one of our original members come back 10 years later!

You probably have a ton of former members that would love to come back.

Why don't you just ask them?

Step one is knowing that list of people and staying in touch with them.

Go through your CRM and build a list of all former members that have the ability to come back to your gym.

This list excludes members you may not want back and members that have moved out of the area.

Once you have the list, it's important to give them a reason to want to come back.

This is where events like 6-week fat-loss challenges are great because there is something specific you can invite these people to attend.

These are highly qualified people and you can contact them in any way you want.

You have their phone number, so you can call them or send a text message.

You can put together a 3-letter direct mail campaign to their physical address,

You can email them.

Hell, you even have their credit card number!

You know what they do for a living, how many kids they have and what sports teams they like.

If they didn't leave unhappy these are some of the most qualified people you could ask for.

The Comeback Video Message

If you want to really stand out and get an old member back, try this:

Send them a personal video message telling them you want them back. Use some humor to get them laughing and simply wait for them to call you.

It's an amazing way to build a stronger relationship. Even if they don't come back, I can assure you they will probably be a sound referral source.

The Stuck-in-a-Rut Client Meeting

Member retention is the biggest indicator of financial success as a gym owner. The gym that keeps the most members and combines that with consistent sales and marketing will crush it.

Having a system to be able to save members that are struggling and looking to quit your gym will put you in rare category.

It's common for most training gyms that have clients in their 30s, 40s and 50s to have issues with members getting stuck in a rut.

These are the prime ages of raising children and life is so

busy for these people. I know because I am one of them.

One of the keys is recognizing the signs when people are frustrated

They will say things like: "if I could just lose those last few pounds" or "things are just so busy I have only been coming once a week."

It's important to arm your trainers to listen to these cues.

I teach our team to be detectives.

We listen very carefully to the words they say.

A few weeks ago, a member walked in and I greeted him with "hey Colin, how are you doing?"

His response: "hanging in there."

This means something is up.

Normal gyms would just say nothing.

Great gyms hear this and pry.

Great gyms hear this and say "what's up? Anything you need?"

So that's the first step in managing reluctant clients.

Many times, it's stuff you can do nothing about.

We have tons of members who are stressed beyond belief taking care of their ailing parents. I know this, too, because I am one of them.
In this case, we just need to be there for them and help

them as best we can.

For the cases where people are legitimately stuck in terms of their progress in the gym, well, that calls for a strategy session.

We have helped several members get back on track using this meeting structure and have retained members when other gyms would have just lost them.

Retention is a massive key to sales and making more money in the fitness industry.

Here's how we do it.

Step 1: Get clear on what their challenge is and help them set a goal.

Most of the time it's a frustration that they are not losing weight, but it could be an injury or just feeling a little burnt out.

It's important to reinforce what they are actually looking to accomplish.

I like the question tell me what success looks like for you in terms of your health and fitness.

Get them talking and then help them formulate a clear goal.

Step 2: Connect them back to their "why."

Connect them back to why it's important for them to get back on track.

I love the question "what's the big reason why you want to

get out of this rut?"

The conversation usually goes to being a role model for their kids or living a long life or helping make a difference in the world.

This links them back to a more important reason of why they need to get in gear.

Step 3: Formulate a simple and easy plan.

It's clear something may need to change. That could be how many times they are training, what they are eating, how they are sleeping or even something else entirely.

Help them determine the things they need to start doing differently to get back on track.

We use something called a health road map to leave them with everything they need to do for their health on one page.

It's been a major contributor to the success of our members.

Step 4: Set a date for another meeting.

Set up another time to check in with them in 1-3 months depending on the situation.

Average gyms just lose these people.

Great gyms help people learn from these experiences and keep people in their system because they know they cannot change their life when they are gone

This is a way to keep members that have a strong potential

to leave your gym and give you a concrete system you can teach to all of your team members to get people back on track.

Members That Want to Quit Due to Financial Hardship

Since our facility is full of uber successful people that live in expensive homes, have lots of kids and a lavish life, it turns their life upside down when they get into financial trouble. Most of time it is losing a job, or maybe their company is struggling.

These people usually just say I need to terminate my membership – they often are too proud to say why.

When a good member terminates for no apparent reason, we always dig and ask why.

When it comes back to stress and financial issues we do whatever we can to help them.

In the past year we have had 2 long time members try to terminate with no reason. After a brief chat, we created a solution and kept them in the gym.

How you handle this is your business, but I have comped people, lowered their membership and the like, and most of them have returned to full paying members very quickly.

My stance is that we will not leave them behind in a time of need and the angle is in stressful times, their fitness is the most important thing to maintain.

This has strengthened our bond with those members and also kept them as clients when they would have otherwise left for good

CHAPTER 10:
CRANKING YOUR CASH FLOW

Every sales book needs to address the cash situation. In a recent poll I saw with a group of gym owners as participants, cash flow was one of their biggest challenges.

Here are a few ways to make sure your cash flow stays full.

Paid in Fulls

When we were moving into our facility this past July, we had a ton of expenses from new equipment to flooring to lawyers, etc.

We wanted to use our own money for the project and not take a loan, so we went to a few of our long-time members and offered them an 8% discount in exchange for their 12-month membership in full.

Many of the gladly did it. It was a win/win.

They were saving money and got the feeling they were helping us open our new gym.

It was great for us that we were able to fund our new facility without any debt. I am not a fan of doing this a lot, and I certainly don't like paid in fulls on a regular basis.

I really think expected monthly income is very important. With that being said, if you're in a bind and you need some cash, this can be effective.

Trim Expenses:

I look very closely at every expense we have. There are always things you can trim. The one thing I never trim is stuff that makes me money.

I won't trim most marketing or business development/ coaching, for example, if it's helping. Why would you trim something that, if used properly, gives you a very high return?

I recently trimmed an online newspaper we advertised in. It was close to $300 per month and we were not seeing a return on that investment. I cut it and we haven't missed a beat.

I changed our email marketing service from Infusion Soft to Active Campaign and saved another $200/month for an easier-to-use service.

Take a close look at all your expenses: I am sure you'll find some free money.

Payroll Percentage of Revenue

Many gym owners do not pay attention to this number.

The typical percentage for a gym is about 20-40% (the sweet spot is 30-35%) of revenue for payroll (owner's draw excluded). So, if your gym revenue is 20K a month, your payroll should be 4-6K a month.

Track this number and if it's high, you may need to make some changes. Not easy stuff, but we must remember that if the business is not healthy, no one is.

Set a Budget.

Most of the time cash flow gets low because we spend

too much money on stuff we don't need. I spend liberally on stuff that makes me money and I am frugal on stuff that doesn't.

Setting a budget at the start of the year and sticking to it is key. Take a look at it monthly – you're either on track or off track.

Here are the things you can really control that you should budget for before January 1st:
- Marketing
- Equipment
- Education
- Business Development
- Meals and Entertainment
- Travel

Re-Think the Athlete Focus

If you want wavering cash flow, then have your bread and butter program be athlete performance training.

I only say this because this was us for a long time. When we changed this, everything got so much better... *especially* our cash flow.

I know so many gyms that have closed or struggle greatly because they focus so much on athletes.

They look at the adults as a side thing, but it should be the other way around if you want to make more money. The bread and butter needs to be the thing that pays you year-round. Let me give you some bad stats.

You will lose 25% of your athletes ever year, even if you do an amazing job! They go to college! Athlete-only gyms are a flawed model if you are using the business

to build a life and not a hobby. The ones that do survive are unicorns and cannot be copied. The worst mistake is modeling your business after a unicorn.

Get a line of credit for your business. If you run into issues, you can always draw on the line and interest rates are very favorable right now. If anything, it provides some peace of mind.

CHAPTER 11:
SALES GOALS

The scoreboard is the most important tool you could possibly use as a gym owner.

It holds key metrics you need to tell if your business is on track or off track.

The scoreboard tells you where to go if there is a problem.

One of the most common complainants I get is that gym owners don't know what to focus on. The scoreboard tells you that.

If you have 10 consultations and only sell 5 trial memberships, those numbers should tell you there is a massive problem with what is happening during your consultations.

If you get 40 leads and only 5 come in for a consultation, there is a massive problem with your lead conversion system.

If you don't know these numbers, you have no clue where to go to fix things.

It shocks me how many guys run their gyms with a blindfold on.

The hard part about this is that what gets measured points directly to the cold, hard truth and many guys would rather fly blind than embrace that.

In terms of marketing and sales, the most important numbers are:

- Leads
- Lead source (i.e. Facebook ad, referrals)
- Consultations Booked
- Consultations Held
- Trials Sold
- Memberships Sold

If you keep track of these numbers on weekly basis you will always be in control of the growth factor for your gym.

Failure to know these numbers is a massive mistake.

Finding the goal for each of these categories is very simple.

Decide on the number of new members you want per month, let's say for simplicity's sake that it's 10.

Double that number and that's how many trials you need to sell – so, 20 trials sold.

Double that and that's how many leads you need (40) to get 10 new members.

This is running at a 50% conversion rate and this is a safe bet but, some gyms will run higher or slightly lower. This serves as a great starting point.

CHAPTER 12:
WHO SHOULD DO SALES FOR YOUR GYM

The owner's most important job is to master sales and marketing.

Here's the reality: without a consistent flow of new leads and contracts, you will always be treading water.

I work with many more gyms that cannot seem to get more leads and new members than those that have problems with retention.

WITH ALL OF THIS BEING SAID:

You must be good at what you do.

If you're not good, then everything catches up to you.

If you have crappy customer service or your training never evolves, or your members never get results, it will be hard to succeed.

Even if you get sales and marketing down, you will be filling a leaking bucket. This is where people run out of money.

So, I'm assuming you have good retention. If you don't, there's a different book on company culture coming for you soon.

The 3 Sales Positions

There are 3 separate positions for the sales role and who does what completely depends on your current structure.

1. Lead Converter: the person the fields the leads and converts them to consultations.

2. Consultation Specialist: the person that holds the consultations and closes meetings.

3. Trial Concierge: the person that keeps in touch with the people on a trial membership.

Lead Converter

Whether you get people on the phone or they come through an opt in, there needs to be someone that owns booking consultations from incoming leads. You can have a few different people that do this, but someone needs to be responsible when, all of the sudden, the conversion rate is down.

This probably should be the owner in the very beginning, but it definitely should be delegated as the business grows. The key is having a strong system is in place that is followed by all.

If you had to use one number to measure the success, I would use a percentage of 50-60%.

Consultation Specialist

As the owner or general manager, you must have your finger on the pulse of everything to do with sales, but the actual consultation is the critical event and must be the last thing given up.

A massive mistake I see is gyms delegating the consultations to inexperienced, untrained sales people.

Simply because a trainer has an open hour to hold a consultation does not put them in a position to help the business grow. In fact, they are often a liability.

Think of all the money you invest in marketing only to see it set on fire when the consultation is garbage because the trainer is untrained and just filling an hour.

One of the last things I gave up before I became a full-time consultant was holding consultations.

I had not trained a soul in years, but I was still the starting pitcher. I got to build a great first impression and put them in the right place. Since my name was on the door and I studied sales, I did well, very well.

If you own your own gym, then you should be the one doing consultations until you find and train someone to be almost as good as you.

If you are looking to get the gym to function fully without you, then you need to find one of your trainers or managers interested in sales, train them on how to do it using this book as a resource and then give them the ball.

We only have 3 coaches that hold consultations and 2 of them do the majority. In order to be selected to hold consultations, they have to participate in a weekly sales meeting to make sure we are following our system and to collaborate about how we can make it better.

The success of this position can be measured by a 90% conversion to a purchased trial and a 50-60% conversion from trial to membership. Note that because the trial is a team effort by many people, it's difficult to put this all on one person if it starts to falter.

The Trial Concierge

As mentioned earlier, the follow-up process with members on a trial is very important. It is scripted, but one person needs to do it.

We've gone back and forth with having multiple people do the follow-up, but it always works better when one does it. It can be an admin or a coach, and it's not a full-time job.

It can be packaged as a stipend for someone looking for more hours. I estimate we have 32 people a month on a trial and it takes them just a few hours a week to perform effective follow-up, and this includes personal phone calls.

Simply introducing the new member to your trial concierge person puts you in a category of your own.

These 3 positions can be done by the same person. It really all depends on your volume of leads. The bigger the volume, the more people you'll need.

Head of Sales

At the end of the day, someone needs to own the results of all 3 sales positions and, in most cases, it's going to be the owner.

The person that is responsible for the success of all 3 positions will also own the job of meeting with struggling members, backend sales and re-activation of old members as these all fall into the sales category.

The main number you use to evaluate this position is the average amount of money people pay per month.

CONCLUSION

So why are sales so important?

Sales are important because sales make money.

Money is the gateway to freedom.

Freedom to live your life on your own terms.

To be able to make decisions simply because you want to.

To design your day to be the perfect day, every day.

To do ONLY the work you love.

To do what you were put on this planet to do.

This is a very powerful thing but, unfortunately, most people never find it.

But you're not like most people.

Most people don't even read books like this.

Most people don't read books at all.

Freedom to be able to help people in need.

Imagine that a family member ran into tough times and you had the finances or free time to be able to help them.

What a feeling of accomplishment to be able to help your loved ones through a jam.

When you're not successful financially you will start to depend on others. Instead of being a lifeline for people, you become a liability.

Freedom to give your family a great life.

Kids are wonderful, but they are very, *very* expensive.

I write a monthly check of $2500 a month just for my 3 kids to go to pre-school, and that's not including any other activities.

College is on the horizon, and weddings – it's a lot when you think about it.

The money I spend taking my kids to go rock climbing, on vacation or to get them a much-needed tutor is some of the most fulfilling money I spend.

How could I look at my son and say I cannot get him extra math help because I was afraid to ask for more money in my gym?

Or that I priced my services so low that there was not enough left to go on a family vacation?

The gym business is NOT easy, but massive success is very possible as a gym owner.

Too many people are quitting too early or are simply accepting a life of mediocrity as a gym owner.

This book provides the building blocks to make a lot of money in the fitness industry.

When you get the sales right, you are a step closer to having a gym that's SPF.

Simple, Profitable and Fun.

Life will be better when your gym is SPF.

Life will be easier when your gym is SPF.

You'll be happier when your gym is SPF.

The right sales process is a key ingredient to making your business SPF and, in turn, it will give you the free, happy and prosperous life you deserve.

Made in the USA
Las Vegas, NV
01 January 2025

15615069R00073